TAKE A WALK ON THE WILD SIDE

DEDAN SAVES THE DAY

BY **THEA FELDMAN**

Animal Planet

© 2006 Discovery Communications, Inc.
Animal Planet and logo are trademarks
of Discovery Communications, Inc.,
used under license. All rights reserved.
www.animalplanet.com

Design by E. Friedman
Contributing consultant Dr. Robert W. Shumaker
of the Great Ape Trust of Iowa

© 2006 by Meredith Corporation.
First Edition. Printed in the USA, bound in Mexico.
All rights reserved.
ISBN: 0-696-23291-X
Meredith® Books
Des Moines, Iowa

Munch, munch, munch! Dedan was hungry. During his morning walk across the hot African savanna, he found a cluster of tasty green leaves at the top of the tallest tree.

Tall Trivia

Giraffes are the world's tallest animals. An adult male, called a bull, can grow to be more than 18 feet! A giraffe's neck can grow to more than 5 feet long!

Dedan paused and turned to look for his young son, Okang who was with his mother, Dalila. Dedan smiled as he watched them playfully nuzzle one another.

Tall Trivia

A baby giraffe, called a calf, is more than five feet tall when it is born! In about 20 minutes most can stand and drink its mother's milk. A mother giraffe is called a cow.

Dedan wrapped his long tongue around a bunch of leaves for one last bite before he moved on. When he turned to go, Dedan made sure that Dalila and Okang were following.

Tall Trivia

A giraffe's tongue is purplish-black in color and can be 18 inches long! The roof of a giraffe's mouth is grooved, which helps strip leaves off branches.

The herd soon stopped in a patch of tall grass. It was a very hot day so they stood still and enjoyed the cool breeze while tickbirds climbed up and down their long necks.

Tall Trivia

Giraffes often have passengers. Little tickbirds eat the ticks and other insects on a giraffe's coat. This is good for both animals: the tickbird eats and the giraffe gets clean!

All of a sudden a strange male giraffe came up to the herd. The stranger wanted to chase Dedan away and take the herd for his own! After Dedan made sure Okang was safe with Dalila, he wrapped his long neck around the stranger and pushed. They pushed and pushed! Dedan was strong but was the other male giraffe stronger?

Tall Trivia

Two male giraffes fight by intertwining their necks and pushing. This shoving match, called "necking," is used to decide who is stronger.

Baby Okang was afraid. Who would win? Who would watch out for him if the stranger chased his father away?

At last Dedan proved he was stronger! He smiled reassuringly at his son, Okang as the intruder galloped off.

Tall Trivia

Giraffes live in groups called herds. A herd has no leader and its members come and go. The average herd has 10 giraffes.

With the excitement over, the herd slowly began to walk and graze. Just when it seemed as if the day would end quietly, Dedan saw something sneaking through the tall grass. What could it be?

Tall Trivia

Giraffes have the largest eyes of any land mammal. They also have excellent vision and as tall as they are, not much blocks their view! Giraffes can see as far as a mile away.

Okang looked up at his father and saw that Dedan was standing stiffly and his tail was twitching. Okang knew that signal meant danger. Dedan had spotted a cheetah! In a flash the herd raced to get away.

Tall Trivia

Giraffes can run up to 35 miles an hour. An adult giraffe's legs can grow to be six feet long and the hooves can be the size of dinner plates!

Because of Dedan's warning, the herd was able to outrun the hungry cheetah. They stopped to rest near a stand of trees. There were thousands of leaves just waiting to be eaten! Dedan nudged Okang closer to some low branches and then Dedan reached out his long tongue and grabbed a mouthful of leaves from the treetop.

Tall Trivia

Giraffes spend most of the day eating. They eat about 75 pounds of leaves, buds, and twigs every day! Their favorite food is the leaves of the acacia tree.

Dedan led the herd to a nearby watering hole. He stood guard while the giraffes spread their long legs and lowered their heads so they could reach the cool water.

Tall Trivia

Giraffes get most of the water they need from the plants they eat. However, if water is available, they can drink up to 10 gallons at one time.

With their bellies full and no danger in sight, the herd walked across the savanna. Seven long necks and horned heads swayed back and forth as a cool breeze blew through the tall grass.

Tall Trivia

A giraffe's coat can vary in color from light tan to black; the difference in color is due to what they eat and where they live.

As another day came to a close, the herd looked for a safe place to spend the night. Okang looked at his father proudly. Dedan fought an intruding giraffe and saved the herd from a cheetah. Dedan had saved the day!